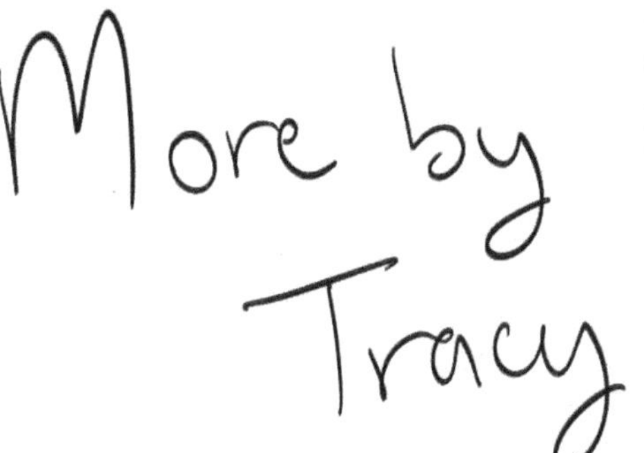

Build a web app using Python + Django!
Written for non-programmers.

https://hellowebbooks.com/learn-django

Learn web design fundamentals and
shortcuts, aimed at non-designers!

https://hellowebbooks.com/learn-design

ME!
@limedaring

BOOK STUFF!
@hellowebbooks

♥ HELLOWEBBOOKS.COM ♥

Hey friends!

My name is Tracy Osborn — I'm the author of Hello Web Books, beginner-friendly videos and books teaching beginner web concepts (https://hellowebbooks.com).

In 2010 I taught myself how to code, and my world just *opened up*. I went from only using what other people built for the computer, to being able to build my own computer widgets and products and even a full-fledged startup. I love being able to code and feel like I can *speak* to computers to tell them what to do.

And, for the learn-to-code journey, learning the "command line" is the first step. It's a really scary step — no helpful graphics or buttons, just a blank space where you can type in commands, and who knows what's going on in the background?

BUT. When you learn *just enough* to work with the command line, which means you can start working with programming languages like Python, believe me: It's not as scary as it might seem.

(This booklet was originally created as an addition to *Hello Web App*, my course/book teaching beginner web app development using Python and Django. Want to learn how to build a web app, maybe an Instagram clone or your own blog system? Check out *Hello Web App*! https://hellowebbooks.com/learn-django)

What is the command line?

We're used to having programs for everything we want to do on the computer. For example, our Finder window, where we can navigate our hard drive, create new files and folders, delete files, and navigate every file we have stored in our system.

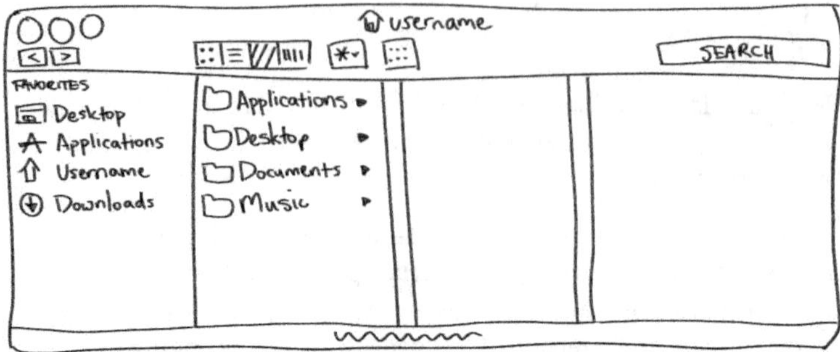

The Finder window, the user interface we use to explore the files on our hard-drive.

We can do the same thing in the command line — navigate our system, see our files, update or change our files — we just won't have a graphical interface (graphical means shiny buttons and dropdowns) on top of what we're doing, and instead of clicking, we have to type out what we want. The default program on the Mac is "Terminal" — open it up and check it out.

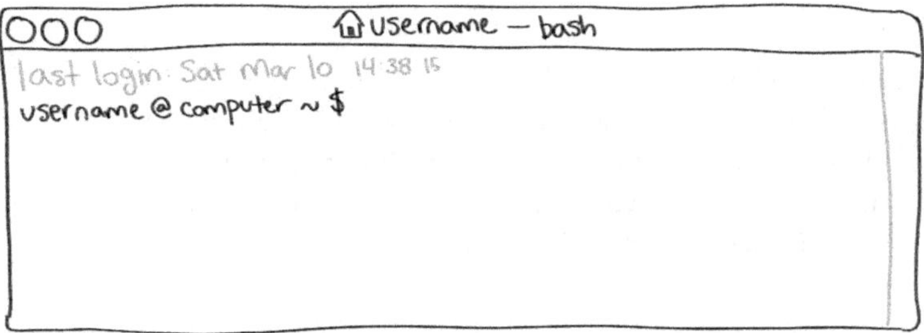

The command line on Mac. Just a blank space to type in.

And yeah, that sucks, we got to remember what to type and what commands we can use. No worries, you don't need to memorize everything! This booklet will teach the easy basics (with a cheat sheet at the end) and you can slowly pick up other commands as you need them during your programming journey.

What is Unix?

You might see other guides teaching the command line mentioning "Unix" a lot. Unix is, essentially, a family of operating systems, which Mac and Linux are a part of. A lot of guides call the command line, the "Unix command line," because Mac, Linux, and other computers share the same set of commands to talk to their computer (so hey, everything you learn here can be used if you ever use Linux!)

The exception is Windows, who decided to do their own slightly different thing. Thankfully, for Windows users, there are a lot of utilities out there that allow you to use the Unix commands on a Windows computer. By and large, programming tutorials and tools assume that you can use Unix commands, so Windows users install additional utilities on the computer.

I'm not going to mention Unix from here on out, but just wanted to give you a heads-up in case you get confused by other tutorials!

How is this tutorial different?

I am going to gloss over most technical details and summarize things into understandable, dumbed-down, explanations. Not saying that you're dumb! A lot of other tutorials get into the mindset of, "Well let's explain *everything* that is going on! The *full, complete, detailed, confusing* explanation so you know *exactly* how things work!"

If you're like me, your mind start glazing over when an explanation gets way too wordy. I don't want to do that here. And to those who might be reading this guide and thinking, "Well, that's not *technically exactly* correct..." — I'm not going for technically exactly. I'm going for *just enough* so you (dear reader) feel comfortable jumping in.

Let's start playing!

The blank, scary command line

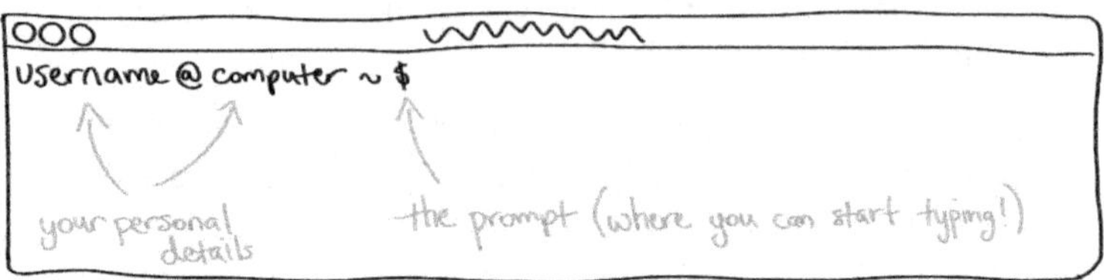

Your username and computer name, and then $ shows you where you start typing.

Back to this blank page with all its hidden power and possibilities!

In the example above, you see my username "limedaring", and my computer name, "Orion," so what you see will be different and will show your own personal values.

The $ is the prompt. In a lot of programming tutorials, you might see commands that you need to type into your command line looking like this:

```
$ yourcommandtotypein
```

These tutorials use that $ to show you that you're in the command line and this is the place where you'll be typing, ignoring your own personal username and computer name.

Listing files in our current directory

```
ls
```

The first command we'll learn is ls, which is short for "list." You will notice that commands are shortened to be as short as possible, which'll be helpful when you're comfortable using these commands and are typing them in over and over. Less characters to type!

Type in `ls` and press enter, and see what happens:

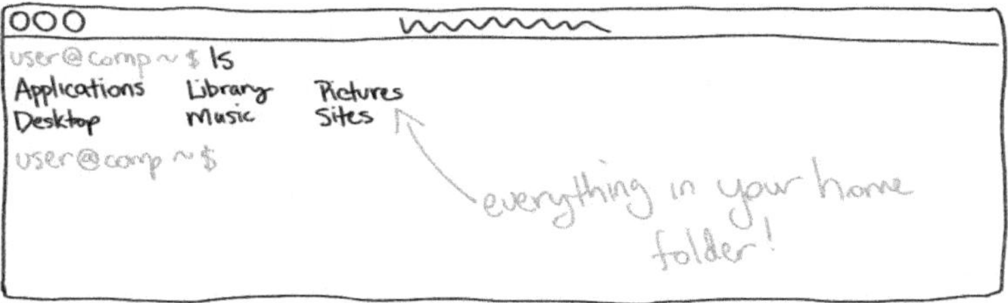

Oh hey, that might look familiar! Open up a new Finder window and click on your username in the left sidebar. It's all the same files/folders!

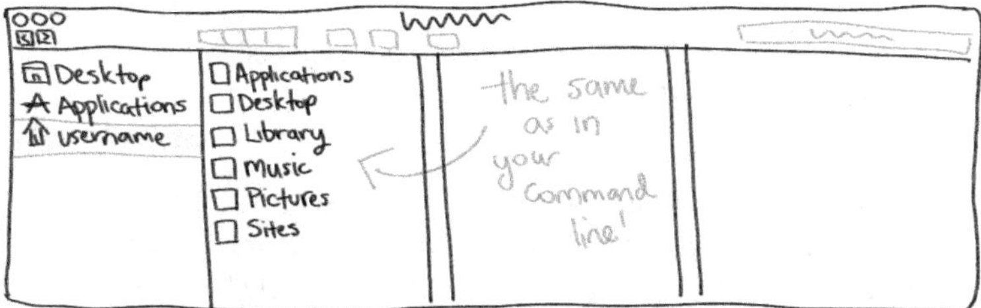

The command line always starts us in our user directory. And just like how you can click on a folder in Finder to see what's in the folder, you can navigate in and out of folders (which we'll refer as "directories" here on out) using your command line.

Changing directories

cd

In Finder, I can click on "Music" see to see the contents of that folder. And in the command line, I can use the command cd ("change directory") to "open" up that directory.

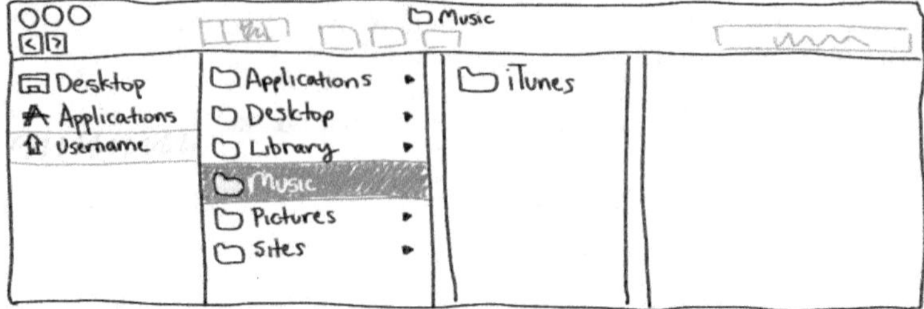

Clicked on Music, I can see the contents of the folder.

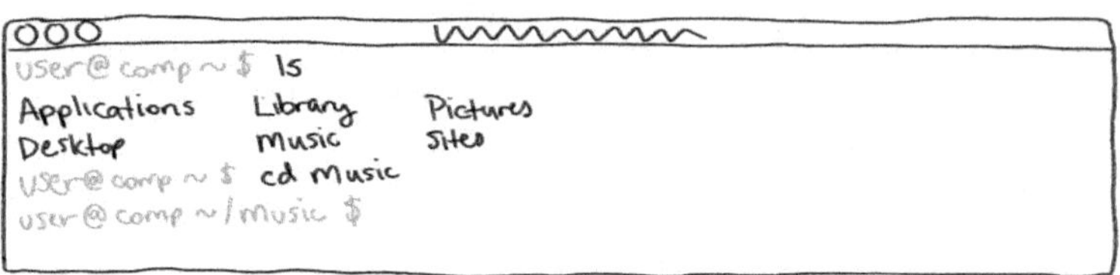

I cd'd into Music. Compared to Finder. Looks kind of boring compared to Finder!

In the command line screenshot, I cd'd into Music. Use your imagination — you just *stepped* into the directory. The command line updated to show that you're currently "in" the Music directory. And here, you can use ls to see the directory's contents, just like in Finder.

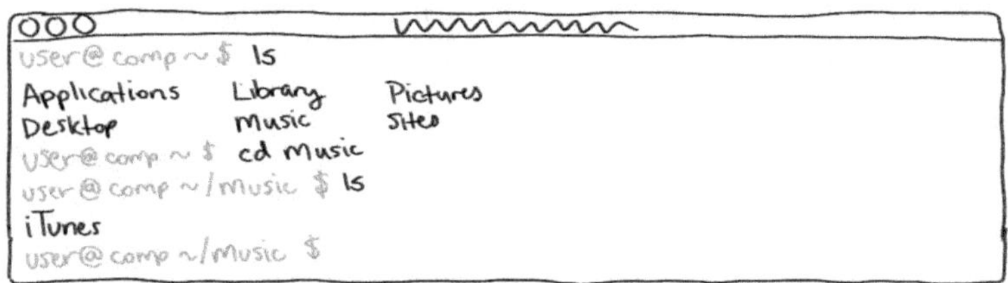

There's that iTunes folder!

In your Finder window, you could click around anywhere and see the contents of those folders. Finder is, essentially, cd-ing and ls-ing behind the scenes, and displaying the results in a much prettier graphical representation, rather than just using text.

We can use `cd` and `ls` again to check out the iTunes directory:

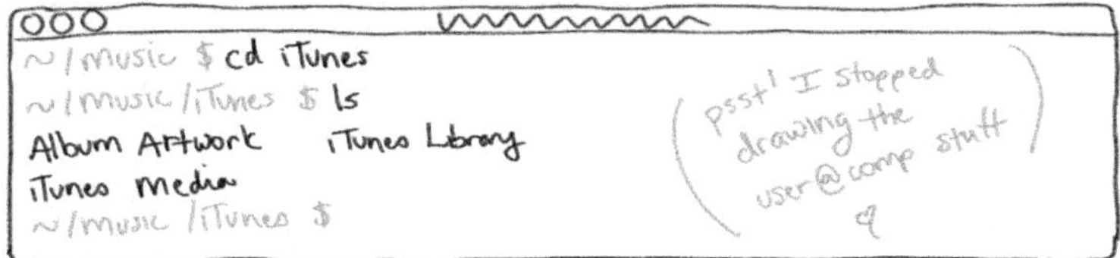

Wait, we're only stepping forward. How can we go back to where we were before?

Changing directories to go back to where we came

`cd ..`

In the command line, we can't just click and go anywhere. It's not even obvious how to go back to our main user directory! For that, we'll use `cd ..` to step back:

We can even chain the dots with a slash to step back multiple steps:

Hey, we're back in that home directory! I like to use `ls` to double check where I am by checking out the contents of the directory.

Go back too much? Use `ls` to see what's in the directory you're in, and then use `cd` to head back to where you want to go:

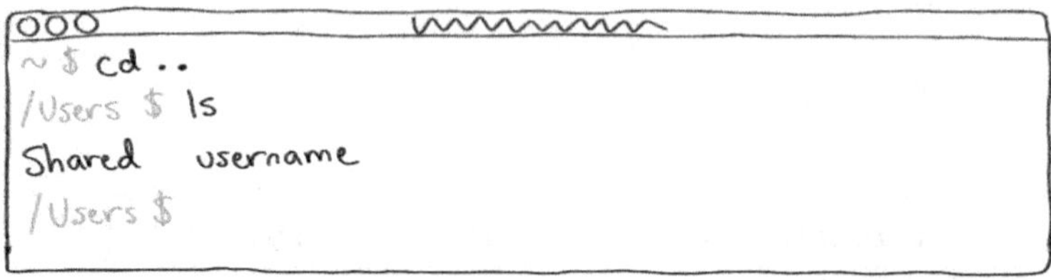

We went "back" too far, now we're in the directory that contains our main user directory.

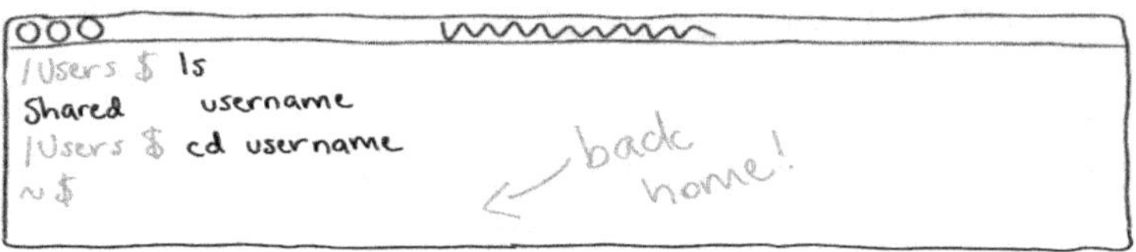

cd into your user directory (using your own username) to get back into your main home directory.

Fun fact! You can `cd` into any folder that you want from Finder by dragging the folder into the command line! This one is a little bit hard to illustrate. You just type `cd` into your command line (don't forget a space after `cd`), then click and hold on a folder in your Finder, and drag it over to where you would type the destination. Your computer will put the path to that folder into your command line for easy cding!

Drag that folder into your command line input area to get the path!

Here's where things start to get fun. We can use the command line to create, move, and delete files on our hard drive!

Creating files

touch

touch will allow you to create files from nothing. Just add the name and type of file you want after the touch command.

Let's make a new file, *hello.txt*. Wherever you want (perhaps in your home directory), type touch hello.txt.

There isn't going to be any success message or anything, so do ls to see the contents of the directory that you're in to confirm that the file was made. Tada!

```
~ $ touch hello.txt
~ $ ls
Applications    hello.txt    Music
Desktop         Library      Pictures
~ $
```

And you can see the file in Finder as well:

Desktop
Applications
username
Downloads
Applications
Desktop
hello.txt
Library
Music
Pictures
new!

Maybe we don't want it in the home directory. Instead of clicking/dragging it in Finder, let's move it to another directory in the command line.

Moving files

mv

The command to move is mv, which looks obvious enough. There are a few other things we need to add to the command so the computer knows what file you want to move and where you want to move it.

To move the file into, say, the Music folder in my home folder, I would type mv NAMEOFFILE WHERETOMOVEIT — so, mv hello.txt Music to move the *hello.txt* file into the Music folder:

Note that, again, you won't get a success message or anything reassuring, so you can ls on the directory that you're on to confirm that it disappeared, then cd into the directory you moved your file into and ls again to confirm that the file now appears in this new directory:

```
~$ mv hello.txt Music
~$ ls
Applications      Library   Pictures       ← not in the home dir anymore!
Desktop           Music     Sites
~$ cd Music
~/Music $ ls
hello.txt   iTunes        ← now in Music!
~/Music $
```

The ../ thing we learned about changing directories backwards, also works to move the file back up a directory too:

```
~/Music $ mv hello.txt ../
~/Music $ ls                    ← no longer in music!
iTunes
~/Music $ cd ..
~$ ls
Applications      hello.txt      Pictures      ← there it is!
Desktop           Library        Music
~$
```

Next, let's learn how to make copies from the command line.

Copying files

`cp`

Another command that looks just like what it does! To copy, you do `cp NAMEOFFILE NEWNAMEOFCOPIEDFILE`. So to copy our *hello.txt* and name the copied file, *goodbye.txt*, we would run this command: `cp hello.txt goodbye.txt`

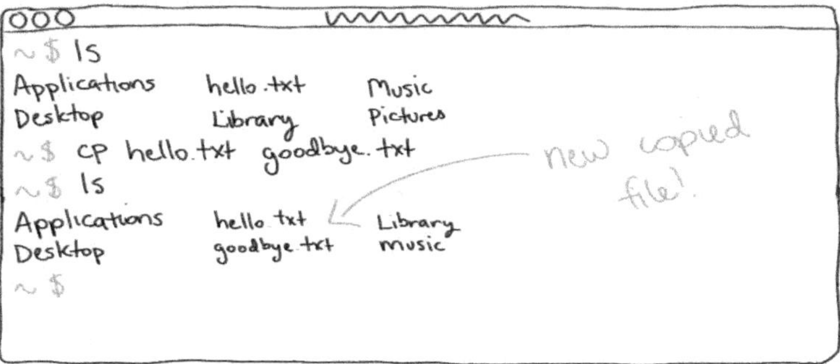

Remember, no response usually *means success!* `ls` *the files in your directory to confirm that the new file has appeared.*

(FYI, if you're looking to copy directories, not individual files, hold your horses — we'll get to that in a bit!)

Kind of silly to have two empty files, right? Let's learn how to delete files.

Deleting files

`rm`

This part is kind of understandably scary. When you delete files using the command line, there is no Trash Can or Recycling Bin for them to live in that you can use to reverse an accidental deletion. They're just gone (eep).

(This is where a system like *git*, a version control system to track changes in files, would comes in handy. It's highly recommended to use with any programming projects so you can save updates and restore from backup if you need to. Stay tuned for a guide for how to work with git!)

We know our *goodbye.txt* file is useless, since it's a copy of our original file (and empty to boot). Let's remove it by using `rm FILENAME` (so, `rm goodbye.txt`):

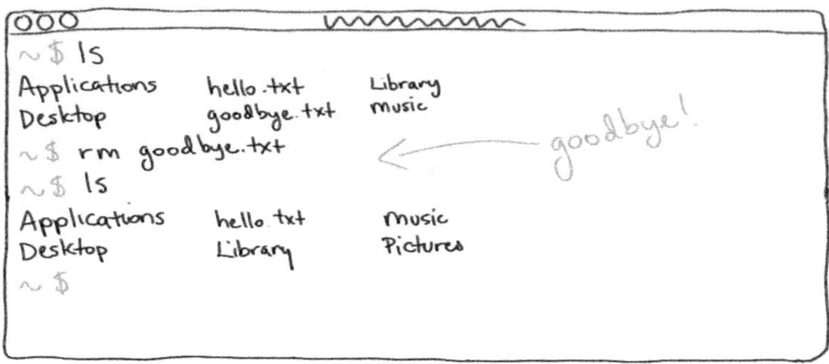

Again, no success message, so we'll check the directories files to confirm that goodbye.txt disappeared.

But I'm tired of typing already!

This whole time I've been having you type everything out (sorry!) There are some nifty autocomplete and other tools you can use to save yourself time when typing commands (or, even better than saving time, preventing typos by using autocomplete.)

Tab to autocomplete

When you're typing a command that involves a file in your current directory (like moving a file from your current directory into another), the command line can auto-complete your file name.

Try it out for moving a file with mv. Remember, the full command is mv `FILENAME WHERETOMOVE` and both of those bits after mv can be autocompleted.

If it doesn't autocomplete (and makes that sad *"doot"* default sound if you have your speakers on), means that autocomplete doesn't see any filenames that start with the letters you've typed so far, so it couldn't find the file or the location you were specified.

This is super handy when you're working with files with long names! After you work with it a bit, tabbing to autocomplete your command line commands will become second nature.

(**Note:** Maybe you typed one character and pressed tab to autocomplete it, and you just get an another *"doot"* from your computer and no autocompletion. That usually means there are multiple files that match what you're autocompleting, so you need to type a bit more until you have enough characters that autocomplete can find the exact file you're looking for!)

Pressing up to access previous commands

If you find yourself typing the same command into the command line over and over (perhaps, down the road, you're running a script you wrote over and over), you can press "up" in the command line to access your previous commands! Hit "enter" after you've found the command you'd like to rerun and it'll execute. Pretty handy time saver.

Intermediate command line utilities

What is sudo?

You might have seen this excellent xkcd comic:

https://www.xkcd.com/149/

sudo is the special secret "I'm the boss and do what I say" com-

mand (and is short for "**su**peruser **do**"). For most commands that affect your computer in a big way (for example, deleting *all* your files, or installing a new program), your computer will require you to put "sudo" in front of it, then require your computer's password, to really make sure that you are aware of what you're doing.

As a beginner, you're not going to need to use sudo very much, but as you continue along in your programming career, you're going to see references to this command.

Making, moving, and deleting full directories

We've been working with individual files so far, but not full directories. The commands we've learned so far — touch (create) mv (move) or cp (copy) for example — won't just work for directories.

Creating directories with `mkdir`

`mkdir` ("**make dir**ectory") is the command you will use to create a new directory. Try making an empty directory named "test" in your current location with `mkdir test`:

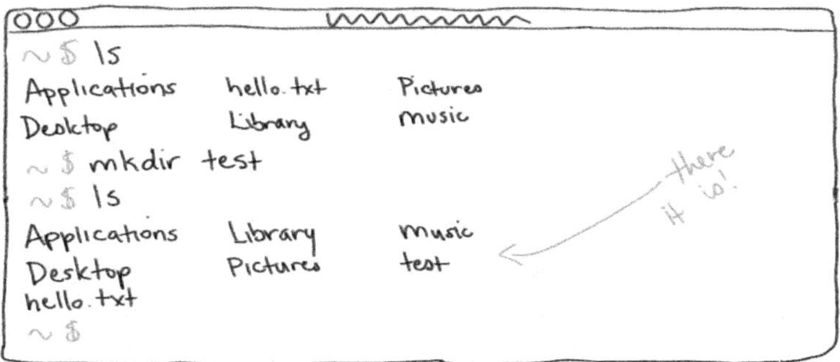

Run `ls` after creating your directory to confirm it was made.

`cd` into your new test directory and, after running ls, you can see that it's empty.

Moving directories with `mv`

This one is just the same as before! Move your new test directory into another other directory with the command `mv NAMEOF-FILE NAMEOFDIRECTORY` (exactly the same as before):

```
~ $ mv test Music
~ $ ls
Applications       hello.txt       Pictures
Desktop            Library         Music
~ $ cd Music
~ /Music $ ls
iTunes      test
~ /Music $
```

Yay, nothing new to remember here. Let's move it back into
our home directory, which would be `mv test ../`. Make sure
you're "in" the directory where you moved your *test* folder.
Also, note that you can move things backwards using the same
`../` notation we learned above for traversing our hard drive!

Let's move our *hello.txt* into our new directory so it's no longer
empty. Go back to your home directory (`cd ..`) and then move
the *test* directory into your currect folder with a "." — so, `mv
Music/test/ .`

Try it out! We'll talk more about the single dot in a few pages.

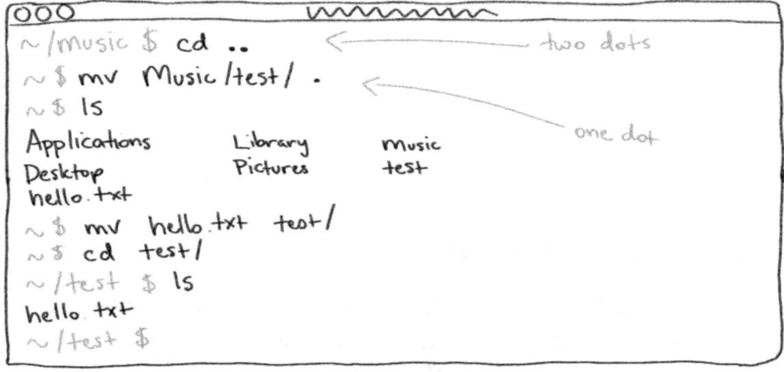

Cool, now we have our test directory with our test file in it!
What happens if we try to delete the whole thing?

Deleting directories with `rm -r`

What's that `-r` thing? New concept alert!

Every command we've learned so far has options (or "flags")
we can add along to the command. We'll explore using a flag
for the first time by deleting our test directory.

First off, try to use our delete command (`rm THINGTODELETE`)
with your test directory. What happens?

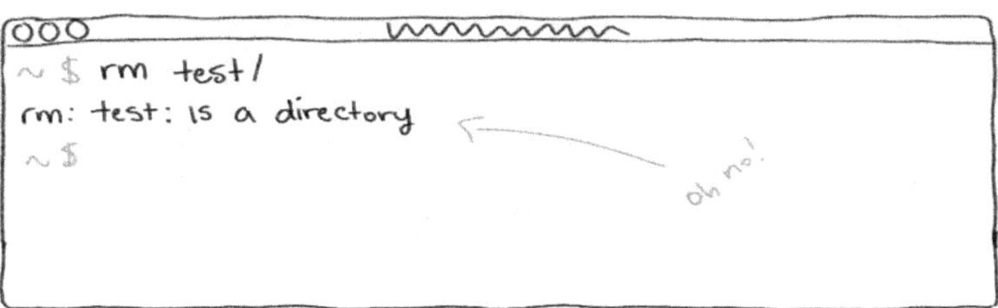

Can't delete the directory because it's a directory! What to do?

When we add `-r` to our command, we're telling it to delete
recursively — so, delete not only the directory but also everything inside it. Without the `-r` flag, the delete fails because the
command line doesn't know if you want to delete *everything* in
the folder. With `-r`, you're basically saying, "Have at it, delete
EVERYTHING" in the directory.

(Fun fact! You might have seen scary things about the command `rm -rf /`. You know the `-r` flag, and you can chain
together many different flags — so here, the `-f` flag is added
too, which means "force." The thing that the command is deleting is `/`, which is the top level directory of your entire hard
drive (which is, usually, your entire computer). So, in english,
this command is "Force remove everything, including directories and all the files, for my entire hard drive." Scary! Back in
the day, you could mess up your computer with just six characters in your command line. Now (yay!), computer makes have
become wise to this and this command will *not* work. No
need to worry about accidentally typing it and wiping your
hard-drive!)

How do I move things *into* my current directory?

Indicating the current directory with .

Once you've gotten comfortable with traversing your hard drive using only commands, you might want to "enter" a directory and then move a file into that directory. So far, we've only covered moving things from the directory that we're in, but we can also move things from elsewhere into our current "location"!

For example, this command: "`mv ../test.txt .`". In english, this is saying "Move *test.txt*, which is the previous directory, into this current directory." That single dot at the end means "current location." Pretty cool!

Using wildcards

When specifying a file, you don't have to be limited to just one — you can use the "*" wildcard to grab multiple files. That sounds confusing. It's easier explained with an example! Say you wanted to move all .txt files in a directory into another directory. This would be the command you'd use:

```
mv *.txt NEWDIRNAME:
```

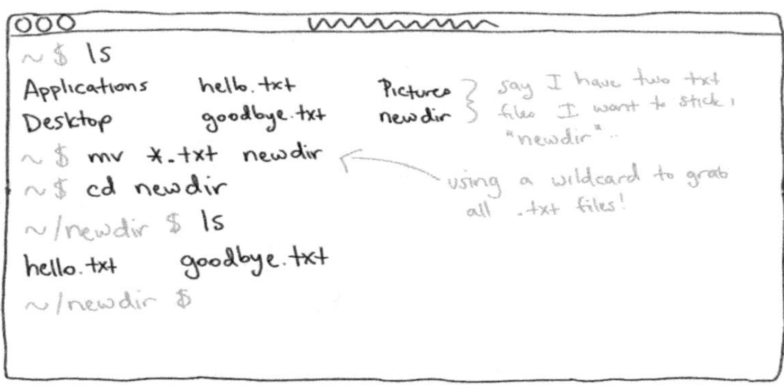

Nifty!

My command didn't work!

Make sure that you're in the correct directory for what you want to run. Often, I'll try to copy a file but forget what directory it is in. Run `ls` (the command to "list" all files in a directory) to confirm that you're in the right directory with the file you need.

I'm stuck and I don't know how to get back to the command line!

Certain commands will replace your current command line window with another interface. Or, maybe you've started writing out some giant command (`mv thisfile.txt to/another/file/folder/wait/not/that/one`) and you don't want to backspace allllll the way back to the start of the line.

Control-C (pressing both buttons at once) is your friend in situations like this. It's basically an escape/start over command that works in most situations to start over. (This is sometimes written as `^C`, because shortcuts are handy.) Note that we're talking the "Control" button here, not "Command!

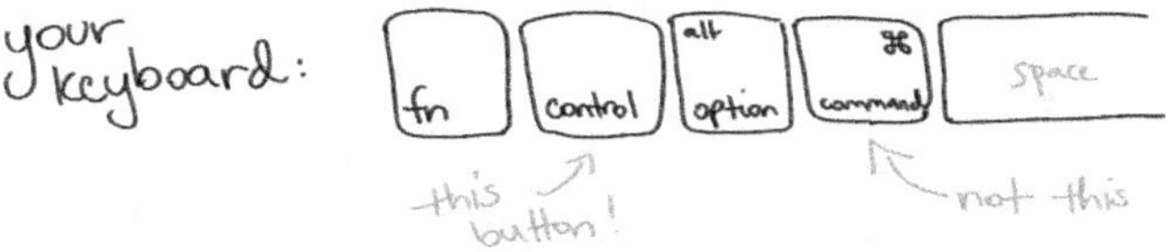

(That didn't work? Try pressing "q", "ESC", or "Control-D." I know this sounds very unspecific but that's what I do when I get into a weird screen that I don't know how to get out of — I mash all the escape commands I can remember. Learn from me, a developer with multiple years of experience!)

I can't see files that start with a dot!

When you're looking in your current directory with `ls`, it's actually showing only *visible files*. Add the flag `-a` ("all") to your command to see every file, including *hidden* files that start with a "."

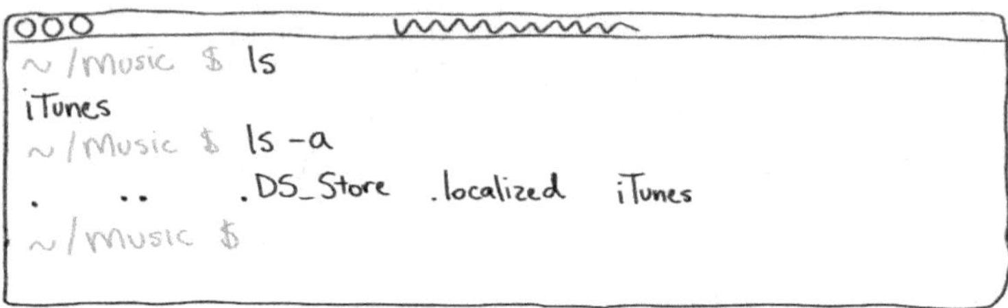

Woah, there are a lot more files in this directory than what it seemed.

Sneaky hidden files! Here's where the command line shines: It's really easy to add the `-a` flag to see all files in a directory, whereas in Finder, it's a lot more difficult to see those hidden files.

What's even sneakier, is adding a `-l` to the command will show you the files as a list, including the timestamps, and owner information, and other useful things. But because it's a list, instead of having three or four or five colours, it's always just one list of file names

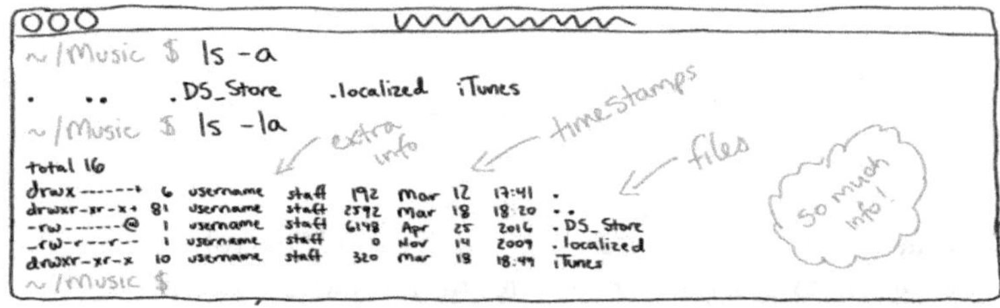

What's even sneakier, is adding a -l to the command will show you the files as a list, including the timestamps, and owner information, and other useful things. But because it's a list,

instead of having three or four or five colours, it's always just
one list of file names

Wow! This is a lot.
You can do it!!

Right? The command line is a *really* powerful tool. We just
skimmed the surface of what you can do, but hopefully covered *just enough* so you feel comfortable poking around and
learning a bit more.

With the command line, you're speaking directly to your
computer — no need for a graphical user interface to translate
for you. And as you go through and learn programming, you'll
find out how much you can do from one little window.

I hope this was a fun introduction for you! Feel free to ask any
questions you have on the *Hello Web App* discussion forum:
https://discuss.hellowebapp.com

If you're looking for the next step, I invite you to check out
Hello Web App, my book and course teaching web app development with Django. Even if you're new to programming and the
command line, the book is pretty easy to just follow along, try
things out, and learn more by doing. Check it out here: https://
hellowebbooks.com/learn-django

Thanks friends, and good luck on your programming journey!

-Tracy

✳ CHEAT SHEET ✳

$ the command prompt
this is where you type!

ls   <u>l</u>ist files in current directory
usually typed all by itself

cd   <u>c</u>hange <u>d</u>irectory
`cd DIRECTORY_NAME`

cd ..   cd backwards a directory
`cd ../`

touch   create a new file
`touch FILENAME.FORMAT`

mv   <u>m</u>o<u>v</u>e file
`mv FILENAME NEWLOCATION`

cp   <u>c</u>opy file
`cp FILENAME NEWFILENAME`

rm   <u>r</u>e<u>m</u>ove file
`rm FILENAME`

rm -r   <u>r</u>e<u>m</u>ove directory
`rm -r DIRECTORYNAME`

sudo   <u>su</u>peruser <u>do</u>
typed at the start of the command to assert that you're the admin

mkdir   <u>m</u>a<u>k</u>e <u>dir</u>ectory
`mkdir DIRECTORYNAME`

pwd   <u>p</u>rint <u>w</u>orking <u>d</u>irectory
show current working directory

utilities

- press tab to autocomplete
- press up to access previous commands.
- "." means "current directory"
- * is a wildcard character

♡ SAY HI! ♡

@hellowebbooks   **hellowebbooks.com**

twitter/instagram   *website*